PH   PTH

SOUND

Sally Morgan

Heinemann
LIBRARY

www.heinemann.co.uk/library
Visit our website to find out more information about Heinemann Library books.

To order:
☎ Phone 44 (0) 1865 888066
📄 Send a fax to 44 (0) 1865 314091
💻 Visit the Heinemann bookshop at www.heinemann.co.uk/library to browse
  our catalogue and order online.

Produced for Heinemann by
 White-Thomson Publishing Ltd.,
Bridgewater Business Centre,
210 High Street, Lewes,
East Sussex BN7 2NH

First published in Great Britain by
Heinemann Library, Halley Court, Jordan Hill,
Oxford OX2 8EJ, part of Pearson Education.
Heinemann is a registered trademark of
Pearson Education Ltd.

Editorial: Sarah Shannon and Harriet Brown
Design: Richard Parker and Flick, Book Design
  and Graphics
Illustrations: Ian Thompson
Picture Research: Amy Sparks
Production: Duncan Gilbert

Originated by Modern Age Repro
Printed and bound in China by South China
  Printing Company Ltd.

ISBN: 978 0 431 08109 0 (hardback)
12 11 10 09 08
10 9 8 7 6 5 4 3 2 1

ISBN: 978 0431 08117 5 (paperback)
13 12 11 10 09
10 9 8 7 6 5 4 3 2 1

British Library Cataloguing in Publication Data
Morgan, Sally
  Sound. – (Physical science in depth)
  534
A full catalogue record for this book is available
from the British Library.

Acknowledgements
The publishers would like to thank the following for
permission to reproduce photographs:
Alamy **pp. 13** (Redferns Music Picture Library),
19 (Danita Delimont), **37** (John Lawrence
Photography), **45** (Lebrecht Music and Arts Photo
Library), **53** (Redferns Music Picture Library);
Corbis **pp. 36** (Amos Nachoum), **39** (Michelle
Pedone/zefa), **40** (Walter Smith); Istockphoto.com
pp. 5 (bluestocking), **14** (Larry St. Pierre), **15**
(Steve Geer), **17** (Norman Chan), **18** (Michelle
Junior), **23** (Jan Tyler), **26** (Oktay Ortakcioglu), **35**
(Moritz von Hacht), **41** (Satu Knape), **46** (Michael
Lynch), **54** (Maartje van Caspel), **55** (Lise Gagne),
57 (Phil Date), **59b** (Kenneth C. Zirkel); NASA
p. 59t; Photolibrary **pp. 21** (Animals Animals/Earth
Scenes), **25** (Animals Animals/Earth Scenes),
29 (Satoshi Kuribayashi), **47** (Norbert Wu);
Science Photo Library **title page** (US Department
of Defense), **7** (Steve Allen), **12** (Andrew Lambert
Photography), **27** (James King-Holmes), **34** (US
Department of Defense), **43** (Pasquale Sorrentino),
50 (GE Medical Systems).

Cover photograph of a jet reproduced with
permission of Science Photo Library (Mehau Kulyk).

Every effort has been made to contact copyright
holders of any material reproduced in this book.
Any omissions will be rectified in subsequent
printings if notice is given to the publishers.

Contents

Words printed in the text in bold, **like this**,
are explained in the glossary.

What is sound?

Sound is everywhere. There are different types of sound, such as the rustling of leaves, the sound of flowing water, the roar of a jet engine, and the sound of a voice. Sound helps to tell us what is happening in the world around us and to enable us to communicate with each other. The study of sound is called **acoustics**.

VIBRATIONS

Sound is a type of energy. Sound is produced when an object **vibrates**. For example, when a drum is struck, the skin of the drum vibrates backwards and forwards, and this moves the air above the drum. When the drum skin moves up, the air is squashed, and when the skin moves down, the air expands, making a sound.

When an object starts vibrating, energy is transferred from the object to the particles in the surrounding air. When the air particles start vibrating, they bump into each other and the energy is transferred from one particle to the next. This causes the sound to spread out in a wave, away from the object.

Compression　　　　　　　　　　　**Rarefaction**

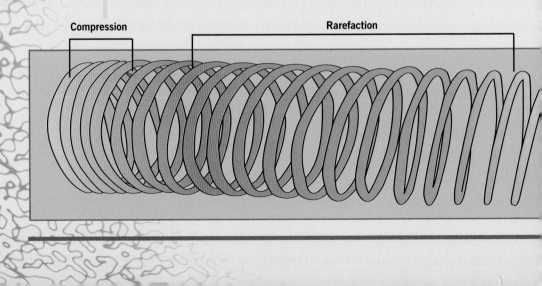

You cannot see sound waves. However, you can imagine how they spread out from a vibrating object by looking at ripples on the surface of water.

MOVING SOUND WAVES

Sound moves in waves which **radiate** out from their source in circles. It's a bit like ripples on a pond that radiate out in ever-increasing circles from the centre. The particles of air in the wave move backwards and forwards in the same direction as the sound is travelling. Imagine a slinky spring on a table. If you push at one end, the coils of the spring push together and then the coils move apart. These bands of **compression** and **rarefaction** move along the spring. This is how a **sound wave** moves through air, water, or solid materials.

Sound needs to travel through a **medium**, such as a gas, a liquid, or a solid. It cannot travel through a **vacuum** (a completely empty space). This is because sound is a form of energy. In order for sound to move it has to transfer its energy from one particle to another. If there are no particles, sound cannot travel.

Compression

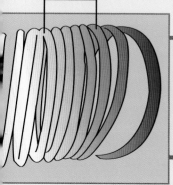

This spring is similar to a sound wave. The areas along the spring where the loops are squashed represent the compressions. In a sound wave, the pressure is much higher in a compression because the particles are close together. The areas of the spring where the loops are stretched out represent rarefactions. In a sound wave, the pressure is lower in a rarefaction.

Sound basics

Sound waves are invisible to us, but they can be represented by a machine called an **oscilloscope**. The shape of a sound wave varies depending on how high or low the sound is, how loud it is, and what is making the sound.

SEEING SOUND

A sound wave is called a **longitudinal** wave because it moves in long, straight lines. A **microphone** in the oscilloscope converts sound waves into an electrical signal. This is displayed on the monitor as a graph. The graph shows the regions of high and low pressure in the wave, called compressions and rarefactions. On the graph, the peaks correspond to the compressions while the troughs correspond to the rarefactions.

It is possible to learn a lot about a sound wave by studying the graph on the oscilloscope. The first thing to notice is the **wavelength** of the sound wave. This is the distance between two peaks or two troughs. The **amplitude** is a measure of the height of a sound wave from the middle of the wave to the trough or peak. The louder the sound, the greater the amplitude (see pages 9–10).

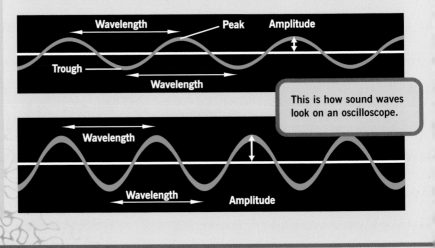

This is how sound waves look on an oscilloscope.

KEY EXPERIMENT Feeling vibrations

You cannot see sound waves as they travel through the air, but you can see and feel their effects. It is easy to feel the **vibrations** created by a sound. Take a cardboard tube and stretch a piece of rubber (from a balloon) across one end and secure it in place with rubber bands. Make sure the balloon is tightly stretched. Hold the tube with your finger lightly touching the rubber. Speak into the open end of the tube and feel for the vibrations on the stretched balloon.

A tuning fork vibrates and produces a sound when it is struck. If the tuning fork is placed in a glass of water, you can see the vibrations moving the water. The tuning fork transfers its energy to the water.

PITCH

There are many different sounds, and one way in which we learn to recognize a sound is by its **pitch**. The term pitch is used to describe how "high" or "low" a sound is. A high-pitched sound is produced by something that is vibrating quickly. The sound waves are close together, or more frequent, so they have a short wavelength. For example, the screech of a bird or the cry of a baby have a high pitch.

Something that is vibrating slowly produces a low-pitched sound, such as the rumble of thunder. The sound waves are further apart and there are fewer sound waves per second. The wavelengths of low-pitched sounds are much longer.

FREQUENCY

The term **frequency** is used to describe the rate at which an object is vibrating. It is measured by counting the number of sound waves that pass a particular point in one second. Objects that are vibrating quickly have a high frequency and they produce high-pitched sounds.

A high-frequency sound also has a short wavelength, whereas a low-frequency sound has a much longer wavelength. The frequency of a sound can be worked out by counting the number of sound waves displayed on an oscilloscope in one second.

Frequency is measured in a unit called a **Hertz (Hz).** For example, 300 Hertz is a frequency of 300 sound waves per second. In other words, the object is vibrating 300 times every second. A 300 Hertz sound is a relatively low-frequency sound. Sound waves in air all travel at the same speed. A higher frequency does not mean that the sound waves are travelling faster – it means that more sound waves are passing a particular spot every second. The sound waves are closer together, not moving faster.

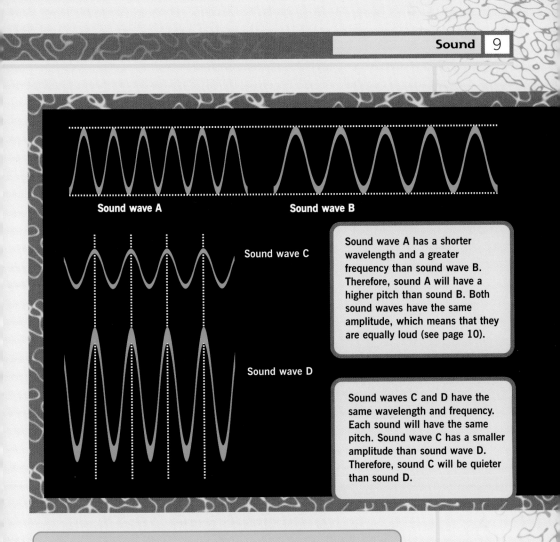

Sound wave A

Sound wave B

Sound wave C

Sound wave A has a shorter wavelength and a greater frequency than sound wave B. Therefore, sound A will have a higher pitch than sound B. Both sound waves have the same amplitude, which means that they are equally loud (see page 10).

Sound wave D

Sound waves C and D have the same wavelength and frequency. Each sound will have the same pitch. Sound wave C has a smaller amplitude than sound wave D. Therefore, sound C will be quieter than sound D.

KEY EXPERIMENT Sound and sound waves

The pitch of a sound depends on its wavelength. You can investigate the link between pitch and wavelength using bottles filled with water. You need six bottles of the same size, each one filled with a different amount of water. Blow across the top of the bottle with the largest amount of water. Blowing across the top causes the air inside the bottle to vibrate and produce a sound. Listen to the sound that is produced. Repeat this with the other bottles. You will find that the bottle with the most water and the shortest column of air produces the highest pitch. This is because this sound wave has the shortest wavelength.

LOUD AND SOFT

Sounds can be loud or soft. The loudness of a sound is a measure of the energy carried by a sound wave. A loud sound has more energy so it causes a bigger vibration and this compresses more particles. This is shown on an oscilloscope as the vertical (up/down) distance between the middle of the sound wave and the peak or trough – the amplitude.

When we make a sound louder, we give the sound more energy so that it vibrates harder. This is called **amplifying** the sound. A loud sound produces a higher peak and a lower trough than a quieter sound. On the graph on page 9, sound wave D will be louder than sound wave C.

Did you know...?

Interestingly, the loudness of a sound gives the impression of affecting its pitch. A loud, high-pitched note seems to sound higher than a sound of the same pitch that is soft. Similarly, a low-pitched note sounds even lower when it is loud. However, in reality the sounds do not change.

KEY EXPERIMENT Twanging ruler

More vibrations mean a higher frequency, so the note has a higher pitch. Fewer vibrations mean a lower frequency, producing a lower-pitched sound. You can learn more about this by carrying out this simple investigation using a ruler. Place the ruler on a table so that about one third of its length sticks out over the edge. Hold the end in place with one hand and twang (flick) the bit that overhangs, so that it produces a sound. Now, move the ruler so that almost all of its length is sticking out, and twang again. Has the sound changed? How has it changed? Try this with rulers of differing lengths and compare the different sounds they produce. Remember that a longer length of ruler produces a lower-frequency sound. See if you can make the sound louder or softer. To make it louder you have to give it more energy so the vibrations are larger.

THE DOPPLER EFFECT

If you listen to the sound of an approaching ambulance siren or of an approaching train, a strange thing happens. The pitch seems to get higher as it moves towards you. Then, as it moves away, the pitch gets lower. The sound seems to change because the object that is producing the sound is moving. As the sound gets nearer, the sound waves are "squashed" together. This means that the frequency is greater and the sound seems to have a higher pitch. As the sound moves away, the sound waves stretch out behind the moving object. The sound waves reach you more slowly, the frequency is lower, and so the siren seems to have a lower pitch.

This strange effect is called the Doppler Effect, named after the Austrian scientist Christian Doppler (1803–53). He carried out various experiments including some involving musicians on trains. The musicians sat on a train and played their instruments while a person stood by the railway line and recorded the notes that were played.

The siren of this moving fire engine is producing sound waves that move out from the fire engine. The sound waves bunch up in front of it and the wavelength decreases. Behind the fire engine, the sound waves spread out and the wavelength increases. As a result, the pitch of the siren changes as it passes by.

Sound waves

Wavelength

Wavelength

Direction of movement

MUSIC AND NOTES

Music is sound that is arranged into notes that have specific pitches and timings. Tuning forks create perfect notes and they are used to help musicians tune their instruments to the right pitch. A tuning fork is a small metal object with two prongs. It is designed to play a note of a single frequency. The length of the tuning fork and the thickness of the prongs are critical as they determine the sound it produces. When a tuning fork is struck against a hard surface, the prongs vibrate and produce a sound of a particular frequency with a specific number of vibrations per second. This is described as a pure sound.

Tuning forks come in sets of eight to produce the notes C, D, E, F, G, A, B, and C. Each letter represents a specific pitch. There are two forks that produce a C. The higher note C has twice the frequency and pitch of the lower note C. This difference in pitch is called an **octave**.

If the sound wave from the tuning fork was displayed on an oscilloscope, the graph would be smooth and regular. This is because the tuning fork produces a pure sound. If the same note was played on a musical instrument the resulting graph would not be quite so regular. A violin, for example, would produce a sound wave that would have the same overall shape, but there would be extra wiggles on the graph. This is because the musical instrument produces a more complicated sound.

This complex sound wave has been produced on an oscilloscope by a violin. The sound wave is less smooth than you would expect with a tuning fork, which produces a pure sound.

KEY EXPERIMENT Investigating tuning forks

You need a set of tuning forks that range in size from small to large. Which tuning fork do you think makes the highest-pitched note? Gently tap the tuning fork against a hard object and listen to the sound. To see if you were right, tap each of the tuning forks in turn and listen to the sound they make.

In an orchestra, the sounds produced by the different instruments go together well. The sounds are pleasant to listen to.

SOUND OR NOISE?

Musical instruments play complicated notes that are made up of a number of frequencies. The frequencies are all related to each other, so they go well together and create a tuneful sound. Noise is a mixture of unrelated frequencies that do not go together. They do not complement each other and do not sound tuneful. When noise is displayed on the monitor of an oscilloscope, the sound wave is uneven and very jagged or spiky.

RESONANCE

Resonance causes a sound to become louder and longer by causing an object to vibrate at exactly the right speed. If you knock an object, it vibrates at a particular frequency and produces a particular sound. For example, when you knock on a door, you get a particular sound. This is the **natural frequency** of the object. The sound is a result of the shape of the object and the material from which it is made.

An object can be forced to vibrate more quickly or more slowly than its natural frequency. Take the example of somebody sitting on a swing. Once the swing is moving, it moves backwards and forwards at its own natural frequency. You can make the swing move further by pushing it to give it more energy. Timing is critical. If you push the swing at the right moment, you give it much more energy and it becomes really easy to keep the swing moving. If you push the swing at the wrong moment, the swing may slow down and you have to work hard to keep it moving. By working in time with the swing, the swing gets larger and larger. In music, the sound gets louder and longer. This is all due to resonance.

Opera singers can shatter a wine glass just by using resonance. The glass shatters because the singer produces a note that is the same as the natural frequency of the glass. This causes too much vibration and the glass shatters.

Resonance is important in the design of musical instruments. When a musician blows on a trumpet, the air within the trumpet is made to **resonate** (vibrate at its natural frequency). This means that the sound becomes louder because it is vibrating harder.

Resonance is essential to play notes of music on a trumpet.

CASE STUDY The Millennium Bridge

When the Millennium Bridge in London, UK, was opened in 2000, so many people walked across the bridge that it started to sway. The swaying was so bad that people had to hang on to the handrail to stop themselves from falling over. The bridge was closed and investigations took place to find out why this had happened. It was discovered that people had started to walk in step with each other and the vibrations of their footsteps matched the natural frequency of the bridge. This caused the bridge to shake. After many months of research the bridge was modified so that it would not sway. It was opened again in 2001.

Alterations were made to the underside of the Millennium Bridge so that it did not sway when people walked across it.

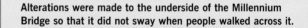

Making sounds

There are many ways of making sounds. Some are as simple as banging a stick against a metal object, while others involve complex musical instruments or even your own **vocal cords**.

MUSICAL INSTRUMENTS

A musical instrument must be able to produce a pleasant sound, and amplify the sound. Many musical instruments have a hollow box incorporated into the design. This allows the air to resonate and the sound is amplified. The sound is also affected by other factors, such as the size of the instrument. A small instrument, such as a viola, produces high-frequency sounds that have short wavelengths, so the notes are high pitched. A cello (a much larger instrument) produces low-frequency sounds that have long wavelengths, so the notes are low pitched.

In some instruments, the musician changes the frequency of the notes by changing the amount of space in which the air can vibrate. For example, a recorder has a series of holes along the length of a tube, which can be covered up to increase or decrease the air space. A smaller space for the air produces a higher-frequency sound.

KEY EXPERIMENT Make a sound box

You can make a simple sound box using a rectangular plastic container without a lid, and six elastic bands of differing thickness. Place the six elastic bands around your box so that they stretch across the open side. Now pluck each elastic band in turn and listen to the sound it makes. How does the thickness of the elastic band affect the sound? Now make another sound box using a smaller rectangular box. Is there any difference in the sound?

There are various types of instrument such as stringed, wind, and percussion. Each type uses a particular method to produce a sound, and each instrument produces a characteristic sound.

STRINGED INSTRUMENTS

Stringed instruments, such as the guitar, harp, or violin, are plucked or played with a bow. The pitch of the note that is produced depends on the length of the string, the tension at which it is held, and the thickness of the string. If the string is pulled tightly to increase the tension, the string can vibrate more quickly, and a higher-frequency note is produced. A thicker string cannot vibrate as quickly as a thin string, so a lower-frequency note is produced. The strings are positioned over a hollow box. This box acts as a resonator to make the sound louder.

A harpist plucks the strings of the harp using three fingers and her thumb. A concert harp has 46 or 47 strings of differing lengths. Each string plays a different note.

Did you know...?

The oldest known musical instruments were discovered by archaeologists in China in 1999. The flutes are made from the bones of birds and are between 7,000 and 9,000 years old.

ELECTRIC GUITARS

Electric guitars are much slimmer than normal guitars because they lack a hollow box. This is because the guitar's sound is amplified by an electrical amplifier and not by the guitar itself. Tiny microphones under each string pick up the sounds and convert them into electrical signals, which are carried to a **loudspeaker**.

SCIENCE PIONEERS Adolph Rickenbacker: The electric guitar

The electric guitar dates back to the early 1930s. Adolph Rickenbacker (1886–1939) is often called the "father of the electric guitar". He was born in Switzerland but lived in the United States. Rickenbacker ran a tool-making company, which made parts for guitars. He joined forces with George Beauchamp and Paul Barth, and in 1931 they made their first electric guitar. It was called the "Flying Pan", and was put into mass production in 1932.

A guitar usually has six strings. The frequency of the note is changed by pushing down on the string with a finger of one hand. This changes the length of the string that is plucked with the fingers of the other hand.

RECENT DEVELOPMENTS New instruments

Musical instruments are still being invented. One of the latest is called the Tritare and it is an odd-looking guitar. It has three necks and six Y-shaped strings. This arrangement of strings allows a greater range of sounds to be played. It was invented by the Department of Mathematics and Statistics of the University of Moncton in Canada.

WIND INSTRUMENTS

Wind instruments, such as the flute and recorder, rely on sounds coming from air trapped in a tube. The different notes are produced by changing the length of the tube. The trombone is slightly different as the length of the column of vibrating air is altered by sliding a length of tube in and out.

PERCUSSION INSTRUMENTS

Drums, xylophones, and cymbals are all examples of percussion instruments. The sound is produced by striking the instrument. The piano is a percussion instrument, too, because the keyboard operates a series of hammers that strike the strings.

An organ consists of pipes of different lengths and a keyboard. By pressing on the keys, air is allowed into the pipes and the sound is produced. The largest pipe organ ever built has over 32,000 pipes.

ANIMAL SOUNDS

Many animals use sound to communicate and they produce this sound in different ways. Humans have a **larynx** (voice box) to make sounds. Birds have a type of larynx called a syrinx. Some insects rub their wings together to make sounds.

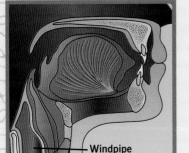

Windpipe

Vocal cords

Windpipe

The human larynx is a hollow, box-like structure that lies in the windpipe. Inside the larynx are two **membranes**, which stick out from the side of the larynx. These are the vocal cords. When air passes over them they vibrate and create sounds. You can feel the vibrations by simply placing your fingers on your larynx and speaking.

When you breathe in and out, the vocal cords are pushed to one side so the air can pass. To speak or sing, the cords move together and block the windpipe. Air pushes past and this makes the cords vibrate. Different sounds can be produced by tightening or relaxing the vocal cords. This alters the pitch of the sounds. The co-ordination of breathing, chest movements, lips, and tongue is also needed to produce precise sounds.

The human larynx is in the windpipe. The two vocal cords lie across the windpipe. Vibrations in the vocal cords produce sounds.

Did you know...?

At puberty, the larynx of a boy gets much larger. A larger larynx has thicker vocal cords and this alters the pitch, so the boy now produces deeper sounds.

Frogs also have a larynx to produce sound. Male frogs can make their croak much louder by inflating a sac under their throat so that it becomes full of air. The sounds resonate around the inflated sac. This enables their croaks to carry over long distances and attract females.

The sound of croaking frogs can be very loud. The croaking attracts female frogs to the pond.

SINGING BIRDS

Birds use sound for communication too – especially song birds. Birds have a syrinx, which is found close to their lungs. This is a large box with many membranes. Air leaves the lungs and passes through the syrinx. Birds produce different sounds by moving the membranes in and out. The size of the bird also alters the sounds. A small bird produces higher-frequency sounds than a larger bird. For example, a tiny wren can produce very high-frequency sounds, while the bittern (a much larger bird) has a deep booming call a bit like a foghorn.

INSECT SOUNDS

Insects do not have a larynx or a syrinx so they use other parts of their body. For example, the grasshopper chirrups by rubbing its spiny thigh against the edge of its wing. Among the noisiest insects is the cicada. Some male cicadas can produce sounds that can be heard nearly half a kilometre (quarter of a mile) away. This insect makes its loud sound by rapidly vibrating a circular membrane on its **abdomen**.

Hearing sounds

Hearing is the sense that detects sound. The ear is a **sense organ** that collects sound and converts it to an electrical signal that is carried to the brain.

THE HUMAN EAR

The human ear consists of three parts – the outer ear, the middle ear, and the inner ear. The outer ear collects and funnels the sound to the middle ear. Between the outer ear and the middle ear is a membrane called the **eardrum**. Sound waves cause the eardrum to vibrate. When the eardrum vibrates, it touches the first of three tiny bones in the middle ear. This bone vibrates and causes the other two bones to vibrate. The movement of these three bones – the hammer, the anvil, and the stirrup – amplifies the vibrations and transfers them to the inner ear. The inner ear consists of a fluid-filled coiled tube, called the **cochlea**, and three semi-circular canals.

Ears are used for hearing and for balance. When you move, fluid in the semi-circular canals moves too and it pushes on cells. These cells send signals to the brain about the position of your head and this helps to keep you balanced.

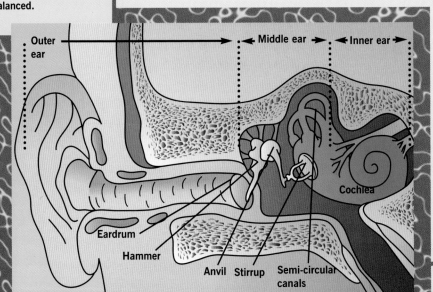

Outer ear

Middle ear

Inner ear

Cochlea

Eardrum

Hammer

Anvil Stirrup Semi-circular canals

There are thousands of tiny **sensory** hairs in the cochlea and they are squashed when the fluid vibrates. This causes electrical signals to be sent along nerves to the brain. The brain interprets these signals as sounds.

Humans have two ears, one on either side of the head. Generally, sound waves reach one ear before the other and this tiny difference in time enables the brain to work out the direction from which the sound came. If the sound comes from in front or behind the head, sound waves reach the ears at the same time. Some animals can move their outer ears and this helps them to pinpoint the source of the sound more accurately. Dogs, for example, can distinguish between sounds that are much closer together than a human can. A barn owl has one ear that is slightly higher than the other and this gives it excellent directional hearing. It also has a particular arrangement of short feathers on its head that creates a heart-shaped face. This funnels sounds towards the ears.

A barn owl's hearing allows it to hear the rustle of small animals as they run along under the grass. The owl's heart-shaped face directs sound towards its ears.

KEY EXPERIMENT Locating sounds

For this experiment you need a friend to help you and a small clock with a loud tick. Blindfold your friend and hold the clock about one metre (3.3 feet) to the side of their head, level with their ear. Ask them to state the position of the clock. Now move the clock to a different position. Can your friend tell where the clock is? Ask your friend to cover one ear and repeat the experiment. Do they find it harder to tell where the clock is located when one ear is covered?

HEARING RANGE

The bigger the outer ears, the more sound can be collected and funnelled into the ears. Some animals, such as rabbits and hares, have extra long outer ears for better hearing. This enables them to hear a **predator** approaching. Humans often cup their hand behind their outer ear to increase its size and improve their hearing.

WHAT CAN HUMANS HEAR?

The lowest frequency sound that humans can hear is about 17–20 Hertz, such as a foghorn. The top end of the hearing range depends on a person's age. A child can hear sounds of a frequency up to about 20,000 Hertz, such as the whine of a midge. However, as a person gets older, the hearing range decreases. It starts decreasing at about 20 years of age. By the age of 70 years it has decreased to about 10,000 Hertz. Older people often accuse other people of mumbling because they cannot make out what they are saying. Due to their hearing loss, they have difficulty in making out certain consonants, especially "s", "f", "t", and "z".

Hearing range varies between different animals. Dogs and cats can hear higher-frequency sounds compared with a human, but they cannot hear the low frequencies so well. Bats and mice can hear even higher frequencies. Elephants can hear low-frequency sounds in the range of about 10 to 10,000 Hertz.

RECENT DEVELOPMENTS The teen buzz

The normal ringtone of a mobile phone is pitched at about 14,000 Hertz. However, teenagers can hear higher-frequency sounds of 17,000 Hertz and above. Now there are ringtones available at a frequency of 17,000 Hertz that are for young ears only! They sound like the buzz of a mosquito and they cannot be heard by adults. Not surprisingly, they are becoming popular among students who do not want their teachers to hear their mobile phones ringing in class.

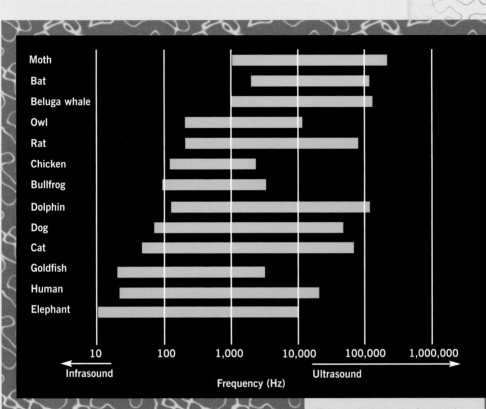

	10	100	1,000	10,000	100,000	1,000,000

Moth
Bat
Beluga whale
Owl
Rat
Chicken
Bullfrog
Dolphin
Dog
Cat
Goldfish
Human
Elephant

← Infrasound   Frequency (Hz)   Ultrasound →

This graph shows the frequencies heard by different animals.

Did you know...?

The kangaroo rat lives in the desert. Its eardrum and middle ear are extra large, while the membrane between the middle and inner ear is extra small. This arrangement enables the animal to amplify sounds by as much as 100 times. Its hearing is so sensitive that it can hear the sound of air flowing over the wing of an owl.

DEAFNESS

Deafness involves the loss of hearing. There are two main causes of hearing loss. One is injury to the outer and middle ear, and the other is damage to the inner ear and nerves.

Loud bangs or explosions may puncture the eardrum, or the ear may be blocked by wax. Sometimes, the ear is malformed due to a birth or **genetic defect**. It is often possible to treat these causes of deafness, for example by repairing the eardrum or by repositioning the three bones in the middle ear.

Deafness due to damage to the inner ear and nerves may be simply due to getting older. Sometimes, however, the nerves can be damaged by an infection, a blow to the head, or by excessive noise (see pages 38–40). Loud noises can damage the sensory cells in the cochlea. The person gets ringing or hissing noises in their ear. This may be temporary but it can become permanent. Nerve-based deafness may be treated with a hearing aid, but sometimes doctors are unable to treat the deafness.

HEARING AID

A hearing aid is a small battery-operated electronic device that is placed either inside or on the outside of the ear. A hearing aid has a tiny microphone and its job is to amplify the sound waves to restore almost normal hearing. However, a hearing aid can only work if the person has some hearing. It cannot help people who have lost their hearing altogether.

A hearing aid fits around and in the ear. It amplifies sound waves to help restore hearing.

The latest hearing aids are **digital**. They collect sounds and process them using a tiny computer within the hearing aid. They can be programmed to deal with different situations, for example to amplify sound more in a quiet environment but to amplify it less in a noisy environment. Some digital hearing aids adjust the amplification automatically, according to the level of noise around the wearer.

RECENT DEVELOPMENTS Cochlear implants

For some people who are completely deaf, a possible treatment is a **cochlear implant**. This bypasses the sensory hairs in the cochlea. The cochlear implant consists of an inner and an outer part. The outer part is worn like a hearing aid. It gathers sounds and converts them to electrical signals. These are carried by a wire to the **transmitter**, which is placed on the head. The transmitter connects with an implanted receiver that is surgically placed inside the head. The inner part of the implant connects the cochlea with the outer part. It allows electrical signals to be carried directly to the nerves.

The part of the cochlear implant around the ear is the microphone. It picks up sounds and sends them to the transmitter – the circular object at the top of the photograph. The receiver is beneath the skin of the scalp. It collects the sounds and sends them to the nerves of the inner ear. The nerves carry electrical signals to the brain.

EXTREME SOUND

Outside of the range of sounds we can hear are very high-frequency sounds called **ultrasound** and very low-frequency sounds called **infrasound**. Although we cannot hear these extreme frequencies, there are some animals that can.

ULTRASOUND

Ultrasound is sound that has a frequency of more than 20,000 Hertz (see page 25). Although humans cannot hear ultrasound, it has a number of uses in modern life. One of the most important is that of ultrasound scanners used by doctors to "see" inside the body (see pages 50–51).

Many animals can hear ultrasound and make good use of it. Among these animals are cats, dogs, bats, dolphins, and moths. Very high-frequency sounds have extremely short wavelengths so the ear of the animal has to be specialized to hear these sounds. Also, high-frequency sounds do not travel very far, so the animal can only hear these sounds if they are produced near by. Another problem is that ultrasound does not have much energy. Animals that hear ultrasound have extra-thin eardrums. If the eardrum was of a normal thickness, the sound waves would be unable to make it vibrate.

Bats can both produce and hear ultrasound. They produce high-pitched squeaks that they use for **echolocation** (see page 46). They also use ultrasound to communicate with other bats. Many bats hunt moths at night. Moths can also hear ultrasound. A moth's ear is found on its body and it can hear the high-pitched squeaks of the bat as it flies around looking for **prey**. Some moths have learnt to react quickly when they hear a bat, by moving very fast away from it! They may fold their wings and drop down to the ground or quickly change direction.

Did you know...?

Noctuid moths are night-flying moths that fly from flower to flower in search of nectar. They are the record breakers in the animal world as they can hear frequencies of up to 240,000 Hertz.

Rodents, such as mice and rats, produce high-pitched squeaks, which they use to communicate with each other. For example, young mice and rats make high-pitched squeaks when they become separated from their mother. Ultrasound does not travel far, so there is less chance of a rodent's squeaks being heard by a predator. Cats, well-known predators of mice, are the exception. They can hear ultrasound and are able to locate a mouse through its squeaks.

This bat is using echolocation to capture the moth.

INFRASOUND

Infrasound is sound with a frequency of approximately 20 Hertz or less (see page 25), which cannot be heard by humans. Although humans cannot hear infrasound, we can feel it. Infrasound is all around us. For example, infrasound is produced by thunder, crashing waves, and vibrating machinery.

If you have ever listened to an organ playing in a cathedral, then you have probably experienced infrasound. It produces a vibrating feeling in your chest. The organ in Sydney Town Hall, Australia, and the Atlantic City Convention Hall, USA, can produce a sound of 8.2 Hertz. Scientists are investigating the effect infrasound has on our mood and behaviour. There have even been concerts that were "soundless" because all of the music was infrasound.

Some animals can hear and make use of infrasound to communicate. For example, elephants produce low-pitched rumbles that can travel over several kilometres, and this allows them to keep in contact with each other. They can also hear the low-pitched sound of thunder, which helps them to find water on wide, open grasslands. Migrating birds may use infrasound to help them navigate because the formations of landscape features, such as mountains and rivers, creates a unique pattern of infrasound that birds learn to identify.

Did you know...?

American biologist Katy Payne (born 1937) was standing near some elephants at a zoo in Oregon, USA, when she felt a throbbing in her chest. She later worked out that the elephants were producing infrasound. Elephants make these sounds to communicate with one another.

RECENT DEVELOPMENTS Can you hear paintings?

New research by scientists at University College London, UK, has shown that the senses of seeing and hearing are linked together in the brain. The research found that people prefer to look at images at the same time as hearing sound. For example, people enjoy ballet with music or films where there is music, rather than looking at just art or listening to music.

Some people have even closer links between these senses and can hear certain sounds when they look at particular images. **Abstract paintings** often contain bold shapes that provoke some people to hear or be reminded of sounds. For example, when looking at an abstract painting, one woman said that a circle made her hear a booming sound, while a series of lines reminded her of steel blades scraping against each other. Other people have said that triangle and boomerang shapes were laughing sounds.

Have a look at this piece of abstract art. What sounds come to mind when you look at each different shape?

Travelling sounds

The speed at which a sound wave travels is called the speed of sound. The actual speed depends on the type of medium the sound is passing through. Sound travels at 340 metres (1,115 feet) per second in air. This means that somebody standing 340 metres (1,115 feet) behind you will hear a sound coming from in front of you one second after you do. Sound travels more quickly through liquid than through gas and even faster through solids. The speed of sound in water is four and a half times faster than in air, at 1,500 metres (4,920 feet) per second.

STATES OF MATTER

The reason that there is a difference in the speed of sound in gas, liquid, and solids is to do with the number and positioning of particles. Air is a gas. In air, the particles are widely separated from each other. They do not bump into each other that often, so the sound vibrations take longer to pass from one particle to another. Also, a lot of the energy is lost as the particles have to move over longer distances.

In a liquid, such as water, the particles are much closer together and so they bump into each other all the time. The particles in solids, such as wood or metal, are tightly held together so vibrations spread even more quickly.

Sound travels most quickly through solids such as metals. For example, when you are standing at a station you often hearing the rails "singing" before you hear the sound of the train arriving. This is because sound travels more quickly along the solid metal rails than through the air.

SPEED OF SOUND IN METRES (FEET) PER SECOND	MEDIUM THROUGH WHICH IT TRAVELS
340 (1,115)	Air
1,500 (4,920)	Water
3,000 (9,840)	Brick
5,000 (16,400)	Metal

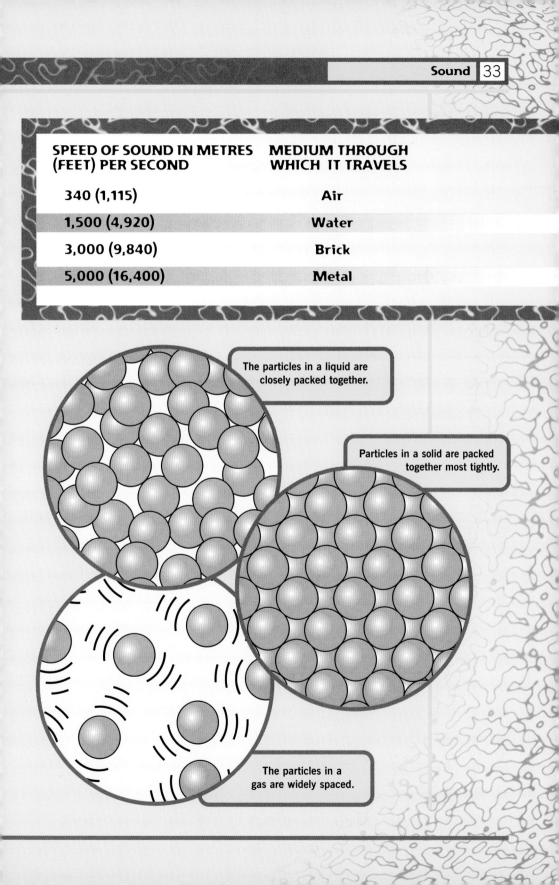

The particles in a liquid are closely packed together.

Particles in a solid are packed together most tightly.

The particles in a gas are widely spaced.

SUPERSONIC SPEEDS

Some aircraft, such as Concorde and some military fighter jets, can fly faster than the speed of sound. When they fly at speeds that exceed the speed of sound, they create a loud bang that is known as a **sonic boom**. This is because the aircraft is travelling more quickly than the sound waves that it is creating. The air moving in front of the aircraft is squeezed so hard that it creates a shock wave that is heard as a sonic boom. Sometimes, the noise and pressure of the sonic boom can damage buildings on the ground. An aircraft that is flying at about 1,200 kilometres (745 miles) per hour, equal to the speed of sound, is said to be flying at **Mach** 1 and if it is flying at twice the speed of sound it is at Mach 2.

This aircraft is travelling at the speed of sound. It has just broken the sound barrier.

Did you know...?

You can work out how far away a thunderstorm is by timing the interval between the flash of lightning and the rumble of thunder. Sound takes about three seconds to travel one kilometre (or five seconds to travel one mile). If the interval was nine seconds, the storm would be three kilometres away (or if the interval was fifteen seconds, the storm would be three miles away).

Next time there is a thunderstorm, try working out how far away the storm is by counting the seconds between the flash of lightning and the rumble of thunder.

EMPTY SPACE

A vacuum is a space where there are no particles. It is a completely empty space. A vacuum can be created by using a pump to suck all of the particles out of a confined space. Sound cannot pass through a vacuum because there are no particles present.

Earth is surrounded by an atmosphere that is full of gases. Sound can travel through the atmosphere. However, beyond Earth's atmosphere is space, and astronomers have discovered that much of space is empty. It is a huge, natural vacuum with no gas particles. This means that sound cannot travel through these regions. However, not all of space is empty. There are regions where there are gas clouds through which sound can travel.

SOUND PIPELINES

Many marine animals use sound for long-distance communication. However, there is a problem with sound in water. Sound may travel more quickly but it does not travel far. This is because the sound is distorted by particles, bubbles, and microscopic life floating in the water. To overcome this, marine mammals, such as whales, make use of a special layer of water at a depth of about 1,500 metres (4,920 feet). The water in this layer is all the same temperature and **salinity**, and it does not mix with the water above or below it. Instead, the water stays as a distinct layer. This layer acts like a pipeline for sounds because any sounds created within this layer of water cannot escape and they stay in the layer over very long distances.

Humans also find this layer of water very useful. The navy, for example, use it to track submarines and other vessels. The navy call it the SOFAR channel, which stands for "SOund Fixing And Ranging channel".

WHALE SONG

Humpback and blue whales make good use of the "sound pipeline". The male humpback whales sing an elaborate song made up of roars, groans, and chirps. Each song lasts a few minutes but then it is repeated over and over again for many hours. The song travels along the "sound pipeline" for hundreds of kilometres.

Unfortunately, the sound pipeline is getting noisy due to all the man-made sounds produced by ships, underwater explosions, and other sound sources. This noise pollution is affecting the way that whales communicate with each other.

The song of the male humpback whale lasts from 10 to 20 minutes, and it is repeated continuously for many hours.

This ship is towing **hydrophones**. These are microphones that are designed to be used in liquid. Scientists can record and study whale song using hydrophones towed in the ocean.

RECENT DEVELOPMENTS Measuring global warming

Global warming is causing the temperature of the oceans to increase. Scientists are using sound to record by how much the temperature of the oceans is increasing. The speed at which sound travels through water depends on the temperature of the water. Sound travels faster in warm water compared with cold water because the particles in warm water move more quickly.

Scientists measure the time it takes sound to travel between two points in the ocean. From that they can work out the average temperature of the water. Their equipment can work out the temperature to within 0.01°C (0.02°F). This experiment is repeated every year to see if there is any change. The project is called ATOC which stands for Acoustic Thermometry of Ocean Climate.

Measuring sounds

The loudness or the intensity of a sound is measured in **decibels (dB)**. The decibel scale ranges from 0 to 180. Humans can just about hear something at 0. Most sounds fall within the 10 to 80 decibel range. For example, two people talking quietly is about 40 decibels, while household machinery, such as a vacuum cleaner, creates a noise of about 70 decibels.

The decibel is an unusual unit because it is measured **logarithmically**. This means that for every increase of 10 units, the intensity of the sound increases by 10 times. For example, a sound of 20 decibels is not double the intensity of a 10 decibel sound, it is 10 times the intensity. A sound level of 30 decibels is 100 times louder than one of 10 decibels.

Level (decibels)	Sound	Effect
0	Quietest sound that it is possible to hear	No damaging effects
10	Breathing	No damaging effects
30	Ticking watch	No damaging effects
40	Quiet conversation	No damaging effects
70	Vacuum cleaner in a room	No damaging effects
90	Pneumatic drill 7 metres (23 feet) away	Prolonged exposure can cause hearing damage
100	Noisy factory	Prolonged exposure can cause hearing damage
120	Loud nightclub/ front row of a rock concert	Sounds become uncomfortable
140	Aircraft 25 metres (82 feet) away	Sounds become painful
160	Rifle fired close to the ear	Eardrum ruptures
180	Launch of a rocket into space	Irreversible hearing loss

A small increase in the number of decibels can mean a considerable increase in the loudness of the sound. Sound intensity can be measured using a device called a decibelometer. This measures the sound waves and converts the pressure reading into a number on the decibel scale.

As the intensity of a sound increases, the amount of time that it can be listened to safely goes down. Most experts agree that for an increase of 5 decibels, the safe exposure time decreases by half. For example, a maximum exposure time of 8 hours is recommended for a sound level of 90 decibels, 4 hours at 98 decibels, and just 2 hours at 100 decibels. Most countries have laws that protect workers being exposed to loud noises. For example, there is often a limit of a 115 decibel sound level for 15 minutes on any day without ear protection. Chainsaws, for example, produce a sound of 115 decibels, so you could only use a chainsaw for 15 minutes a day before the sound levels became unsafe.

Young musicians may like to play their music very loud, but unless they protect their ears they could suffer from deafness later in life.

Did you know...?

If you worked in a factory, the noise levels would be carefully monitored. It would be illegal for the sound to reach 120 decibels for more than a few minutes. However, it is possible to produce similar sound levels by turning up the volume on an **MP3** player! Using an MP3 player at full volume can cause deafness because of the loud sound being so close to the ear.

This official waving the chequered flag at the side of the race track is wearing ear protectors because the noise made by racing cars could damage his hearing.

IS SOUND DANGEROUS?

Sound can be dangerous. People are often unaware that listening to loud music or being in a noisy place for too long can harm their hearing. Loud noises cause deafness by damaging the three tiny bones in the middle ear. These bones are held in the correct position by muscles. A loud noise can cause the bones to vibrate too much and this damages the muscles. Once damaged, they do not work properly while they recover. This is why you cannot hear very well when you come out of a noisy concert. Your hearing recovers over the next few hours. However, ears can be permanently damaged by continual exposure to loud noises. Unfortunately, noise-induced deafness is gradual and a person may not notice that their hearing is slowly getting worse.

How do you know if the noise is dangerous? If you have to shout to make yourself heard, then the noise level may harm your ears. If the noise makes your ears ring or you have difficulty in hearing for a few hours, the noise level was too high.

EAR PROTECTION

People need to wear ear protectors if the sound level at their workplace exceeds 85 decibels. This includes people who operate noisy machinery on a building site or in a factory, work close to aircraft at airports, or work at a concert venue. Ear protection may be in the form of an ear plug that is inserted into the ear canal, or ear muffs. Ear muffs are made from a material that deadens sounds. The material is shaped into cushions that fit around the ear.

The choice of ear protection depends on the type of noise. Ear plugs can be tricky to fit so are worn when the noise level is constantly high. The workers fit the ear plugs at the start of a work shift and remove them at the end. If the noise is intermittent, ear muffs are worn as they are easier to put on and take off.

Musicians also have to protect their ears. Musicians may not want to wear ear protectors because they need to hear the music. They can use specially designed ear plugs that are moulded to fit inside their ear. These ear plugs reduce the sound to a safe level, but do not eliminate it completely.

It is estimated that as many as five million young people in the United States have some degree of damage to their hearing caused by listening to loud music.

DEADENING SOUNDS

Since sound can be harmful, it is important to try and muffle sounds in the home or in the workplace. Also, sound can be very annoying. People do not like having to listen to the noise coming from concerts and parties, or through the wall from a neighbouring home. Usually just the low frequencies can be heard, which are the most annoying sounds. Sounds can be deadened or muffled by using **soundproofing**.

KEY EXPERIMENT Absorbing vibrations

In this experiment you can investigate different materials to see which ones deaden sound and which amplify sound. You will need a clock that has an alarm that you can set off. Take a selection of materials such as cork tile, carpet tile, a piece of wood, cardboard, and paper. Place the ringing alarm clock on each of the materials in turn. Which is the best material for absorbing the vibrations of the ringing alarm clock?

SOUNDPROOFING

Soundproofing works by reducing the vibrations and this reduces the sounds. Lightweight materials that are full of air spaces are good for soundproofing because air does not carry sound very well. For example, foam rubber and **insulation** are placed in the walls and roof spaces of buildings. Double glazing also reduces sound.

Another good way of soundproofing is to lay thick carpets and put up heavy curtains. Carpets and curtains absorb and deaden sounds. In contrast, wooden floors, which are popular in homes, are very good at transmitting the vibrations, so sound carries well through a wooden floor. Wooden floors often cause problems in blocks of flats because the sound of somebody walking across the floor in heeled shoes carries to the flat below.

Some materials are specially made for soundproofing. These materials are full of air-filled spaces, just like insulation.

Special acoustic tiles can be put on walls and ceilings to reduce the transmission of sound. The surface of the tiles may be shaped so that the sound waves are bounced back into the room.

A SILENT ROOM

The ultimate silent room is an **anechoic chamber**, which is completely soundproofed so that no sound can enter. The walls are muffled with tiles so that sound within the room cannot bounce. The room is used to test noise generation from equipment, acoustic instruments, and microphones.

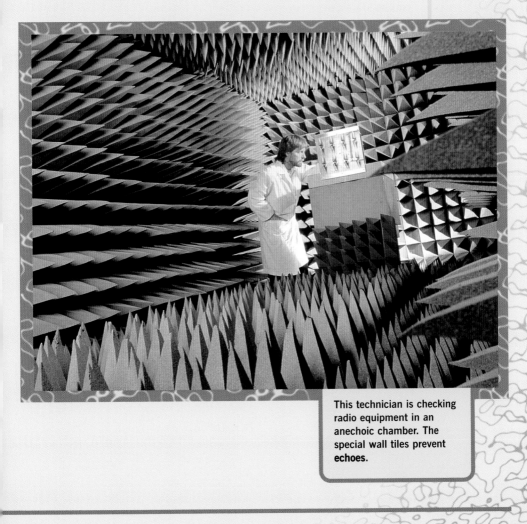

This technician is checking radio equipment in an anechoic chamber. The special wall tiles prevent **echoes.**

Using echoes

Echoes are reflections of sound waves. If you drop a stone in a well, you will hear the sound of the stone plopping into the water repeating in the well for several seconds. If you shout in a tunnel, you will hear the sound of your voice bouncing off the walls. In mountains, sounds bounce around the mountain peaks.

Echoes occur because sound waves bounce off hard surfaces such as walls. The sounds are said to **reverberate**. An empty room with a wooden floor will sound very "echoey" because of the hard surfaces. Shiny surfaces are good at reflecting sounds, too, but fabrics absorb sound waves. In a room, carpets and curtains help to soften the echoes.

ECHOES IN CONCERT HALLS

In a concert hall, the quality of the sound is critical and a lot of careful design goes into the acoustics. Everybody sitting in a concert hall needs to be able to hear, regardless of where they are sitting.

However, it is important not to eliminate all the echoes because the echoes help to create a rich sound. A concert hall that is completely echo-free would sound quite lifeless. Reverberation in a concert hall continues the sound after the note has been played. Most concert halls are designed to have a reverberation of about one or two seconds. If the echoes carry on for any longer, the quality of the sound would be reduced. If you look up in a concert hall you will see an array of sound reflectors and boxes hanging down from the ceiling. They are designed to reflect the sound from the stage down to the audience.

KEY EXPERIMENT Echoes and distances

Echoes are useful for working out distances. Next time you are walking in the mountains, or near some cliffs on the beach, try this simple experiment. Stand some distance from the cliff. Shout loudly and then count or time the number of seconds that elapse before you hear the echo. You know that sound travels at 340 metres (1,115 feet) per second, so multiply the number of seconds by 340 (1,115) and then divide by two. This will give you your distance from the wall in metres (feet).

These saucer-like devices have been suspended from the ceiling of the Royal Albert Hall in London to improve the acoustics of the concert hall.

ECHOLOCATION

Echoes are put to good use by both animals and people. Bats and dolphins combine echoes and ultrasound to navigate and find food. People use echoes and ultrasound to examine the insides of the body (see pages 50–51).

Bats use echolocation to navigate in the dark with great accuracy. They produce a series of high-frequency clicks, either from their mouth or nose. The sound waves travel through the air and bounce off any object in their path. Bats have large ears that they use to pick up any returning echoes, and then their brain processes all of the information. Bats can work out both the size and position of any object in their path. If a bat comes across an interesting object, it will bombard it with sound waves. More clicks mean that more echoes are produced and this gives the bat a more detailed sound map of the object.

Did you know...?

Bats also make use of the Doppler Effect when hunting (see page 11). They work out the speed and direction of their prey from listening to the change in the frequency of the echo.

Bats' ears are perfect for collecting sound waves. Bats use sound to locate their prey.

Dolphins use a similar system. A dolphin produces a series of high-frequency clicks that travel as a beam of sound through the water. The sound bounces off any object in its path. The dolphin listens for any echoes. Echolocation enables dolphins to find fish in murky water and to avoid colliding with underwater objects.

Dolphins use echolocation to help them hunt and catch fish.

Animals use ultrasound for navigation because the high-frequency sound waves do not carry as much energy as low-frequency sounds. This means that the sound waves do not spread out much, enabling bats and dolphins to produce a narrow beam of sound. Also high-frequency sounds have a short wavelength (see pages 8–9) and this means that they can bounce off very small objects that are just a fraction of a millimetre in length.

PROTECTING THEIR OWN EARS

Bats emit particularly loud clicks to find objects that are further away. However, bats have incredibly sensitive hearing and these loud clicks could actually damage their own ears! To stop this from happening, the moment they make the click, a muscle in the middle ear pulls one of the three bones out of the way so that the vibration of the eardrum is not carried to the inner ear. The muscle relaxes and the bone returns to its normal position. Fortunately, the echo from this loud click is much quieter and no damage is done.

SONAR

During the early part of the 20th century, scientists developed an underwater navigation system based on the dolphin's form of echolocation. It was called **sonar**, which is an abbreviation for SOund, NAvigation, and Ranging. A transmitter emits a beam of sound waves, which is sent into the water. When the sound waves strike an object, they are reflected and the echoes are picked up by a device, called a **transducer**, that converts sound waves into electrical signals. These electrical signals are amplified and the information displayed on a monitor. The distance of the object in the water is calculated from the speed of sound in water and the time taken for the echo to return.

There are two types of sonar. A passive sonar just listens for sounds in the water created by ships, submarines, and marine life. It can tell whether something is present or absent but not how far away it is. Many submarines have a database of sounds to enable them to identify the different types of ships and submarines. An active sonar creates a pulse of sound, called a "ping", and then listens for the echo. Active sonar has a number of uses, for example as an echo sounder that sends a pulse of sound directly down to the seabed. It measures the time it takes the echo to return and then works out the depth of the seabed. This can help to tell how far away objects are.

SCIENCE PIONEERS Lewis Nixon: Sonar

The first passive sonar devices were invented in 1906 by American naval architect, Lewis Nixon (1861–1940). He used them to listen for icebergs. Then, in 1915, French physicist Paul Langevin (1872–1946) and the Russian electrical engineer Constantin Chilowski worked together to develop the first active sonar device for detecting submarines. Today, sonar is very common and is used by many people, including fishermen, ocean explorers, and the military.

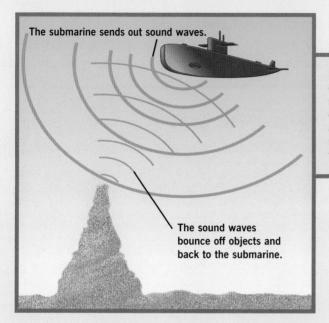

The submarine sends out sound waves.

Sound waves are being sent out by this submarine. The sound waves bounce off objects that they meet, such as the ocean floor, and a series of sound waves return to the submarine.

The sound waves bounce off objects and back to the submarine.

Modern sonar systems can be used to study shoals of fish. Sound waves travel differently through the body of a fish because it has an air-filled swim bladder, and this creates an echo. This means that the sonar can work out the size of the shoal and the direction in which the fish are swimming. Net sounders can be fitted to fishing nets. These devices send sound waves into the net where they bounce off any fish present, creating echoes. The echoes are picked up and the information used to work out the number of fish in the net. This tells the fishermen in the **trawler** when the nets are full and ready to be hauled in.

Did you know...?

Some military sonars are incredibly powerful and produce a loud sound that travels over hundreds of kilometres. These sonars are believed to be harming marine mammals by confusing them and causing them to lose their way. It may even cause whales to swim into shallow water and become beached.

ULTRASOUND AND MEDICINE

Ultrasound scanners use echoes and ultrasound to examine internal structures. They are very common in hospitals, but they are also used by engineers.

SCANNING THE BODY

The ultrasounds used to scan the body are produced by a crystal that vibrates incredibly quickly to produce high-frequency sound waves of between one million and 20 million Hertz. The beam of sound waves is directed into the body. As the sound waves pass through the body, they meet the surfaces of different tissues. The surfaces reflect the sound waves, and the resulting echoes are detected by a microphone. The microphone converts the echoes into electrical signals that are displayed on a monitor as a "picture" of the inside of the body.

This type of scanner allows doctors to examine the internal structures of the body without having to carry out an operation.

The latest ultrasound scanners produce a three-dimensional image of the body, giving doctors an even clearer view. This is a three-dimensional view of an unborn baby.

Ultrasound is also ideal for examining an unborn baby, and all the evidence we have suggests that the baby is completely unharmed by the procedure.

Ultrasound can also be used to scan the abdomen for cancerous and other unusual growths, or to check if an organ is abnormally large. Doctors can check large arteries and veins to see if they are blocked, or scan joints, muscles, and ligaments for injury.

TREATING WITH ULTRASOUND

Ultrasound is also used to treat some medical conditions. Some people suffer from kidney stones. These are build-ups of a hard material in the kidney. The "stones" may be small, just the size of a grain of rice, or as large as a pebble. Kidney stones can be incredibly painful, so treatment is urgent.

Today, a doctor uses an ultrasound scanner to locate and then destroy the stone without having to operate. A beam of ultrasound is focussed on the stone and the energy in the sound waves breaks the stone into many small fragments. These fragments pass out of the kidney with the urine.

CASE STUDY Ultrasound and engineeering

Ultrasound has many uses in engineering, including the detection of flaws in metals. Sound waves can pass through a solid and the speed at which they travel can be measured. If the sound waves meet a crack or a bubble in the metal, the sound waves may be deflected and this shows up on the ultrasound. The first ultrasound metal flaw detectors were developed after the Second World War and now ultrasound scanners can detect the tiniest of flaws. These scanners allow engineers to do internal checks on important pieces of equipment and enable repairs to be made before a piece of metal fails completely.

Recording and transmitting

Producing a sound is useful, but it is even more useful to be able to transmit that sound over a long distance and to record the sound. Sound recording dates back to 1877 when American scientist, Thomas Edison (1847–1931), made the first sound recording on a **vinyl** record. Today, sound is recorded on to CDs and DVDs.

RECORDING SOUND

To record sound, a microphone is used to pick up sound waves and convert them into electrical signals. Inside a microphone is a thin plastic or metal membrane attached to a tube. Wire is coiled around the tube and placed inside a **magnet**. When sound waves hit the membrane they cause it to vibrate. This moves the tube, which in turn causes the coil of wire to move. The coil moves in and out of the **magnetic field** created by the magnet. This movement causes an electric current to be produced in the wire. Quiet sounds do not cause much movement, so the electric current is small. Loud sounds produce a bigger vibration, more movement, and a larger electrical current.

Sound waves cause the membrane to vibrate. This moves a coil, and the coil produces an electric current. The electric signals are recorded on a tape or disc.

Magnet

Sound waves

Membrane

Coils of wire

These electrical signals can be transmitted or recorded, **encoded**, and stored on a tape or CD. To play back the recorded sounds, the encoded data is read and converted into electrical signals that are fed into a loudspeaker.

LOUDSPEAKERS

A loudspeaker is the reverse of a microphone because electrical signals are converted to sound waves. Inside the loudspeaker is a magnet and a coil of wire. An electric current flows along the coil of wire in a magnetic field. This causes the coil of wire to move. The wire is attached to a small paper cone and this is moved backwards and forwards. The movement of the cone creates waves in the air that people hear as sounds. The greater the electric current, the greater the movement, and the louder the sound.

A sound-recording studio will use a number of microphones in the sound-recording room, each recording a particular voice or instrument. The electrical signals are carried to the mixing desk where all the soundtracks are put together.

RECENT DEVELOPMENTS All-round sound recording

The problem with a recording of a concert is that when you play it you do not really get the sense of being there. The sound comes from one direction, while in reality the sounds would converge on your head from all directions. Now there is a new technique of gathering sound information called motion-tracked binaural. The new equipment uses 24 microphones attached to a ball that represents the head. The microphones pick up sounds around the "head". When the recording is played, the sounds appear to come from all directions. This new technique may have many new uses such as on games consoles, in home cinemas, and for teleconferences.

RADIO COMMUNICATION

Radios are used to transmit sounds over long distances. A radio has two parts – a transmitter and a receiver. A microphone picks up the sound and converts it to an electrical signal. Then, the electrical signals are converted to radio waves. A radio wave is an invisible form of **radiation**, just like light. The frequency of the radio waves varies according to the strength of the electrical signal. The transmitter sends out the radio waves, which are picked up by receivers. The receivers have to be tuned in to receive radio waves of specific wavelengths. The radio wave is converted back into an electrical signal and then into a sound.

DIGITAL SOUNDS

Until about 20 years ago, sounds were recorded on to vinyl records or tapes. These methods are called **analogue** processes because the data is a stream of continuously varying signals. Then digital sound recording arrived. Digital data does not vary continuously, it is either on or off. One way to compare analogue with digital is to think of a watch with hands and a watch that displays the time in numerals. The hands of the analogue watch move all the time, but the numbers on a digital watch change suddenly.

CDs and DVDs store information digitally.

Digital sound recording takes the electrical signals from the microphone and converts them into a series of **binary** numbers of 0 and 1. The sequence of numbers is recorded as tiny pits on the surface of a CD by a **laser**. To play back the sound, the CD is placed in a CD player and a laser scans the surface of the CD, picking up reflections from the pits. The digital data is read and converted back into an electrical signal and then into a sound wave.

THE TELEPHONE

The microphone is also part of a telephone. The first working telephone appeared in 1876. Today, the telephone is an essential piece of equipment, allowing instant communication with almost any part of the world.

A telephone is basically a microphone and a loudspeaker. When you talk into the mouthpiece, the sounds cause a thin membrane of metal or plastic to vibrate. Underneath the membrane is an **electrode**, which is connected to a coil of wire. When the membrane vibrates, an electric current forms in the wire. The size of the current depends on the vibrations created by the person speaking. The electric current is carried along a wire to another telephone. There, the signal is converted into sound by the loudspeaker in the earpiece.

When you use a telephone, sound waves are converted into electrical signals, which are carried along wires that connect with the telephone network, enabling you to speak to somebody who may be on the other side of the world.

MOBILE COMMUNICATION

A mobile phone is a cross between a normal land telephone and a radio. When you speak into a mobile phone, the sound waves are converted into radio waves. These are transmitted to the nearest base station. Here, the call is transferred through the telephone network to the base station closest to the phone of the person you are calling. That base station sends out radio waves that are picked up by the phone you are calling and converted to sound waves.

A lot can be learnt about a person from their mobile phone. Their choice of phone, their ringtone, and the graphics they display on the **interface** all say something about the person using the phone. Also, when the mobile phone is switched on, it gives away their location. New technologies are allowing advertising companies to send text messages to mobile phone users in certain areas. For example, a text about a local restaurant can be sent to mobile phone users within 200 metres (660 feet) of the restaurant. New "buddy" services alert you when you are close to any of your friends, while employers can track their employees during the working day.

SCIENCE PIONEERS Alexander Graham Bell: The telephone

Scottish scientist, Alexander Graham Bell (1847–1922), was fascinated by sound. In 1870 he moved to North America where he carried out experiments into converting sound into electricity. Finally, in 1875, he made a receiver that could change sound into electrical signals. Other scientists were working on this problem, too, including American engineer Elisha Gray (1835–1901) and Italian inventor Antonio Meucci (1808–96) but it was Bell who, in 1876, managed to develop his telephone and file his **patent** first. This has proved to be one of the most valuable patents ever awarded and Bell became a very rich man.

KEY EXPERIMENT Make a string telephone

You can make a very simple telephone using two plastic cups and a length of string. Make a hole in the bottom of each of the cups. Tie a knot in one end of the string and thread the string through the hole in the bottom of one cup. The knot will stop the end going through. Now thread the end of the string through the hole in the other cup, going up through the hole from the bottom. Make a knot in this end of the string. Get a friend to hold one cup while you hold the other cup. Pull the string tight. When you speak into the cup, get your friend to listen with the other cup. You should find that the vibrations carry down the string. What is the longest length of string you can use and the telephone still work? Are metal cans better than plastic cups?

Mobile phone use has taken off massively over the last 10 years. Between 80 and 90 percent of the world's population have mobile phone coverage.

Future sounds

Sound technology is improving all the time, and scientists are finding new uses for sound. There are some exciting developments in the fields of medicine, **astronomy**, and even in military weapons systems.

BIONIC EARS

Cochlear implants are expensive and tricky to put in place, so researchers are trying to build a tiny mechanical cochlea from micro-parts and tiny circuits, which could be much easier to implant. This artificial cochlea would have a much greater hearing range than natural ears, giving the person much improved hearing.

Going one step further, there is an experimental brain implant. This implant would bypass the ear all together. An external receiver would pick up the sound waves and send electrical signals directly to the part of the brain that interprets sound.

SOUNDING OUT THE SUN

Astronomers are very excited by new research that is using sound waves to investigate what is going on below the surface of the Sun. Astronomers are analysing sound waves that have passed through the centre of the Sun. The sound waves travel at different speeds through liquids and gases, and are distorted by activities such as earthquakes and eruptions. The results have shown that there are huge clouds of gas moving under the surface, occasionally bubbling to the surface as eruptions.

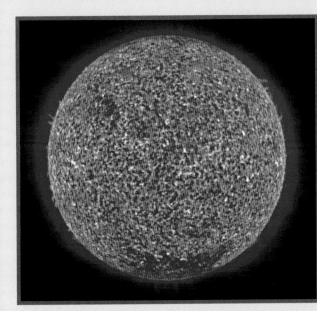

Although astronomers have studied the Sun for many years using powerful telescopes, it was the use of sound that enabled them to learn about the processes taking place beneath the Sun's surface.

SOUND AS A WEAPON

Sound can also be used as a weapon. The United States army has already used a sound weapon in Iraq. The weapon produces a narrow beam of intense sound of up to 150 decibels, which is used to disperse riots. This sound is incredibly painful and people are forced to move away. In future, ultrasound could be used as a weapon. Ultrasound can pass through bricks, concrete, and metal. Such a weapon could produce a beam of ultrasound that would pass through walls and other barriers to harm people inside. The building and its contents would remain unharmed, but a person inside would be injured.

In the future, sound could be used as a weapon.

Further resources

MORE BOOKS TO READ

Focus on Sound, Barbara Taylor (Franklin Watts, 2003)

Light and Sound, Chris Oxlade (Hodder Wayland, 2005)

Making Waves: Sound, Steve Parker (Heinemann Library, 2004)

Sound, Steve Parker (Heinemann Library, 2006)

Sound, Bobbi Searle (Franklin Watts, 2002)

USING THE INTERNET

Explore the Internet to find out more about sound. You can use a search engine, such as www.yahooligans.com or www.google.com, and type in keywords such as sound wave, hearing, resonance, pitch, amplitude, decibel, ears, or frequency.

These search tips will help you find useful websites more quickly:

• Know exactly what you want to find out about first.

• Use only a few important keywords in a search, putting the most relevant words first.

• Be precise. Only use names of people, places, or things.

Glossary

abdomen   hind part of the body of an insect, the lower part of the body of a mammal

abstract painting   art that does not show objects as they appear in the world around us

acoustics   relating to the study or science of sound

amplify   make vibrations larger and make sound louder

amplitude   height of a sound wave from the middle of the wave to the peak or trough

analogue   information that changes continuously, such as the hands on a watch, whereas digital information is in the form of ones and zeroes

anechoic chamber   room that does not let sound waves bounce, so there are no echoes. It is used to test equipment and soundproofing materials.

astronomy   scientific study of the universe

binary   numerical code based on ones and zeroes

cochlea   coiled, fluid-filled tube in the inner ear

cochlear implant   type of hearing aid, part of which is inserted under the skin of the scalp

compression   area of a sound wave where particles are squashed together and the pressure is higher than normal

deafness   inability to hear, complete or partial loss of hearing

decibel (dB)   measure of the loudness of sound

digital   electronic information stored as a series of ones and zeroes

eardrum   membrane between the outer and middle ear

echo   bouncing back or reflection of sound

echolocation   navigation using the reflection of sound

electrode   conductor of electricity

encode   convert sound waves into a code

frequency   number of vibrations in one second. Rapid vibrations have high frequencies and produce high-pitched sounds.

genetic defect   disease or disorder that is inherited from the parents

Hertz (Hz)   unit of frequency

hydrophone   underwater microphone

infrasound   very low-frequency sounds

insulation   substance that does not let sound pass through it well

interface   connection or link between two systems, for example the hardware and software parts of a computer. It is also the term used to describe the appearance or layout of a computer program on a screen, the part with which the user interacts.

larynx   voice box found in the windpipe of a human. It is used to make sound.

laser   beam of intense light

logarithmically   method of arranging numbers so that a large range of values can be fitted on the same scale

longitudinal   running lengthwise

loudspeaker   device that converts electrical signals into sound

Mach   indicates how speed relates to the speed of sound. Mach 1 is the speed of sound and Mach 2 is twice the speed of sound.

magnet   piece of metal (usually iron or steel) that attracts other pieces of iron and steel

magnetic field   invisible force that surrounds a magnet

medium   type of substance through which sound can pass

membrane   very thin sheet of material or tissue

microphone   device that changes sound into electrical signals

MP3   computer file that stores high-quality sound in a small amount of space

natural frequency   speed at which an object vibrates when it is struck

octave   series of eight notes, the top note has twice the pitch of the bottom note

oscilloscope   device that can display a graph of a sound wave on a monitor

patent   official document that states who owns the rights to an invention or idea

pitch   tone of a sound, whether it is high or low, depending on the frequency of the sound

predator   animal that hunts other animals for food

prey   animal that is hunted and eaten by other animals

radiate   spread out from a central point

radiation   form of energy

rarefaction   area of a sound wave where particles are more spread out and pressure is lower than normal

resonance   vibration in an object caused by the vibration of another object

resonate   vibrate and become louder as a result of another vibration

reverberate   bounce sound off walls within a confined space

rodent   small gnawing mammal, such as a rat, mouse, or squirrel

salinity   measure of the salt content of water

sense organ   part of the body that can detect the outside world. The nose, skin, ears, eyes, and tongue are sense organs.

sensory   related to the sense organs or sensations

sonar   system that assists navigation and can locate objects in water. The letters stand for SOund, NAvigation, and Ranging.

sonic boom   shock wave created by an object, such as an aircraft, travelling faster than the speed of sound

soundproofing   method of reducing the spread of sound

sound wave   waves of air pressure differences caused by a vibrating object

transducer   device for transferring energy from one form to another

transmitter   device that converts sound waves into radio waves

trawler   fishing vessel

ultrasound   very high-frequency sound

vacuum   space in which there is nothing

vibrate   shake, or move backwards and forwards, very quickly

vibration   shaking, or moving backwards and forwards, very quickly

vinyl   type of plastic

vocal cords   folds of the lining of the larynx that can vibrate and make sound when air passes over them

wavelength   distance between the peak (or trough) of one sound wave and the peak (or trough) of the next sound wave

Index